Birds of Prey

A Look at Daytime Raptors

Sneed B. Collard III

Watts LIBRARY

Franklin Watts
A Division of Grolier Publishing
New York • London • Hong Kong • Sydney
Danbury, Connecticut

To Mike Harrington and Craig Himmelwright, my favorite highflyers.

The author would especially like to thank the following
"raptor fanatics" for helping make this book fly:
Kate Davis, Bill Muñoz, and Ron Therriault.

Note to readers: Definitions for words in boldface can be found in the
Glossary at the back of this book.

Photographs ©: A. B. Sheldon: 18; BBC Natural History Unit: 48; Cornell Laboratory
of Ornithology: 36 (Robert E. Barber), 3 top, 34 (L.Page Brown), 3 bottom, 13 (Frank
Schleicher); Craig Himmelwright: 43, 46; David Case: 28; Kate Davis: 10, 33, 64; Morris
Myerowitz: 7, 17; Sneed B. Collard III: 8, 12, 31, 39; The Academy of Natural Sciences
of Philedelphia: 9 (P. Davey/VIREO), 20 (Steven Holt/VIREO), 35 (M.P. Kahl/VIREO);
Tony Stone Images: 45 (Steve Bly), 40 (James Martin), cover (Gary Vestal); Wm. Munoz:
4, 14, 16, 21, 23, 25, 26, 27.

Visit Franklin Watts on the Internet at:
http://publishing.grolier.com

Library of Congress Cataloging-in-Publication Data

Collard, Sneed B.
    Birds of prey: a look at daytime raptors / by Sneed B. Collard III
        p.   cm.— (Watts Library)
    Includes bibliographical references and index.
    Summary: Discusses the physical features and behavior of daytime raptors, including
eagles, harriers, kites, Old World vultures, caracaras, and falcons.
    ISBN 0-531-20363-8 (lib.bdg.)   0-531-16419-5 (pbk.)
    1. Falconiformes—Juvenile literature.   [1. Birds of prey]
I. Title. II. Series
QL696.F3C645   1999
598.9—dc21   98-38196
                                                         CIP
                                                         AC

GROLIER
PUBLISHING

Contents

America's second-largest raptor, the bald eagle, can often be spotted along rivers hunting fish.

Raptor Revelation

It was 1984, and I'd just landed a job working on the Pitt River in northern California. I went up and down the river taking water temperatures and measuring how much water flowed in different places. This work was part of a study to find out whether the river could be managed in a way that would allow the number of eagles and trout living there to increase.

A group of **raptor** biologists was working on the same study. At first, I thought they were crazy. Every morning, they'd get up before dawn and drive to some remote spot on the river. They would sit there all day just staring through their binoculars, hoping to see a bald eagle catch a fish. "What a boring job," I thought.

After a couple of weeks, however, I started talking to these people, and they began teaching me about the eagles they studied. One day they took me with them to **band** a young bald eagle. Banding helps biologists keep track of birds. Bands are special tags with numbers on them. Biologists place bands around the legs of eagles and other birds so that they can identify individual birds as they move or **migrate** from one place to another.

Using ropes, my new friends climbed to an eagle's nest at the top of a tall tree and carefully lowered a young bald eagle in a potato sack. After weighing and measuring the bird, they placed a numbered band on its leg.

Before returning the eagle to its nest, however, they set it on the ground. I sat down next to it. The eagle didn't quite know what to make of me. Standing more than 24 inches (60 centimeters) tall, it stared at me with its enormous brown eyes and cocked its sharply curved beak from one side to the other. As I studied its smooth feathers and massive feet, I could feel my attitude toward birds change. Suddenly I realized that I was sitting next to one of the most skilled, beautiful, intelligent creatures I'd ever met. Since that day, I have been fascinated by birds and especially by eagles, hawks, and falcons. Scientists call these birds raptors or **birds of prey**.

Chapter One

Sky Lords

Raptors are often the first birds that attract our interest. That's not hard to understand. Many raptors are bigger than other kinds of birds. Raptors are easier to see and, because only a few different kinds live in a specific area, they often are easier to identify.

But there's more to our fascination with raptors than size. For thousands of years, people have admired and respected raptors. Ancient Romans and Egyptians featured birds of prey

Raptor Relations

The word "raptor" comes from a Latin words meaning "robber" and "seize" or "grab."

in paintings and in mosaics—beautiful scenes made of tiles. Dozens of nations, including the United States, have placed raptors on flags, coins, and art. For people throughout the ages, raptors have represented qualities we would like to have—speed, strength, intelligence, and bravery. But what is a raptor?

There are two groups of raptors. One is the "nighttime raptors," which consists of the owls. The other group is the "daytime raptors," which includes 300 kinds of eagles, hawks, falcons, kites, and vultures. Both groups are fascinating, but

The rough-legged hawk is one type of daytime raptor.

this book focuses on the daytime raptors—the raptors you are most likely to see. Just to make things simple, on the following pages, the word "raptor" refers only to these daytime birds of prey.

Raptor Classification

Scientists often change how they group different kinds of birds and other animals. Currently, scientists divide the daytime raptors into three families.

- One family includes eagles, hawks, kites, harriers, ospreys, and Old World vultures. This is the largest family of daytime raptors. It includes more than 200 different kinds, or **species** of birds.
- The second family includes about 60 species of raptors known as caracaras and falcons.
- The third family includes only a single species of raptor—the secretary bird.

As a group, these three families of daytime raptors display some amazing features and habits. But figuring out exactly what makes a bird a raptor is easier said than done.

Secretary Birds

Secretary birds live only in Africa and are best known for running—not flying—after their prey. Secretary birds eat insects, small mammals, birds, and venomous snakes, which they try to kill by kicking them. **Ornithologists**—people who study birds—believe that secretary birds mate for life. They build large nests in acacia trees and add to the nests year after year. Because secretary birds look and behave differently from other daytime raptors, scientists aren't absolutely sure that they should be placed in this group. Until people learn more about raptor relationships, however, that is where secretary birds will stay.

The peregrine falcon is one of the world's most awesome and respected raptors. Its curved beak is perfect for cutting and tearing flesh.

Chapter Two

Being a Good Raptor

At first glance, different raptors seem to have little in common. Some are as small as pigeons, while others weigh as much as 18 pounds (8 kilograms) and fly on wings up to 10 feet (3 meters) wide. Different raptors eat very different kinds of food and live in very different places—from tropical rain forests to deserts to the Arctic tundra. Despite these differences, all raptors share some important characteristics.

Beaks and Feet

If you look at an eagle, a falcon, or any other raptor, you can tell right away that it is a meat-eater. Almost all raptors have sharp curved beaks that are good for tearing flesh. Their powerful jaw muscles help these birds rip apart dead animals and, in the case of falcons, kill their prey.

Raptors also have impressive feet designed for catching and killing prey. Raptor feet have four toes that are perfect for grasping, with three toes pointing forward and one toe pointing back. The deadly claws, or **talons,** on each toe help many raptors kill their victims by piercing, or stabbing, internal organs. Strong muscles in their legs and feet help raptors hang on to their prey, whether on the ground, in the water, or in the air.

12

Flight Masters

Raptors are famous for being terrific fliers, but their "flight specifications" vary greatly. Eagles and buteo hawks excel at soaring. Their long, wide wings catch breezes and columns of warm air, known as **thermals,** rising from Earth's surface. Falcons and accipiter hawks, on the other hand, have "faster" wings designed for pursuing prey at high speeds.

A raptor's large primary feathers, located at the ends of its wings, help provide the bird with plenty of lift. Most raptors also have powerful flight muscles attached to a large **sternum,** or breastbone. In many cases, these muscles enable the birds to carry prey almost as large as themselves.

The eyes of most raptors point forward more than the eyes of other birds, allowing them to see both to the front and to the sides. The birds' large eyes are packed with sensory cells that take in a huge amount of visual

Raptors are skillful fliers. This red-tailed hawk's broad wings allow it to ride thermal updrafts as the bird scans the ground for prey.

13

information—much more than our own eyes gather. Behind each raptor eye, a complex network of nerves helps the birds process visual information at an incredible speed, allowing raptors to locate and track fast-moving prey. The muscles in their eyes allow raptors to focus on objects much more quickly than mammals can.

Behaving Like a Bird of Prey

Raptor behavior varies tremendously, but raptors do some things alike. Most raptors hunt, but will not hesitate to eat **carrion**—the meat of dead animals—when it is available. Raptors usually mate for life. When they choose a mate, males and females sometimes go through breathtaking courtship displays, twisting and twirling through the air like acrobats and even "locking talons" while tumbling toward the earth. Once they have bonded, or chosen

All raptors, including this red-tailed hawk, are meat-eaters. They must hunt or scavenge prey to survive.

each other, a raptor pair often breeds and nests together year after year until one of them dies.

When they breed, raptors raise few young. Depending on the species, a raptor female lays up to five or six eggs. Often only one or two chicks survive to adulthood—especially among large raptors such as eagles. Female raptors are almost always larger than males, but both parents invest a huge amount of energy in protecting and bringing food to their **offspring**. When the chicks are very young, the female guards the nest and the male brings most of the food. Later, the female joins in the hunting. Just how birds of prey obtain food, though, is one of the behaviors that sets different raptors apart.

Raptor Lifespan

Large raptors usually live longer than smaller ones. A bald eagle can live up to 21 years in the wild, while a kestrel rarely reaches its fourth birthday.

Raptor Hunting

Raptors hunt in an amazing variety of ways. A small falcon such as a kestrel may perch on a tree branch or a telephone wire until it sees another bird or insect fly by. Then it quickly takes off after its prey, slamming into its victim with open feet. Golden eagles often fly close to the ground while searching for a rabbit or squirrel to pounce on. Black-shouldered kites are among the craziest-looking hunters. They hover in one spot over fields and open spaces, flapping their wings rapidly until they "parachute" down on a small mammal or reptile. Other raptors use different hunting methods, as you will see in later chapters.

Picking Out Prey

As a group, raptors have a poor sense of smell and taste, but their keen eyesight has impressed humans for centuries. Raptor eyes point slightly forward, allowing them to see both forward and to the sides as they hunt. Raptors can pick out objects from farther away than we can. An Australian wedge-tailed eagle can spot a rabbit from about 1 mile (1.5 kilometers) away, about three times farther than a person can. They also see more colors than we do—an advantage in detecting **camouflaged** prey.

Raptors on the Go

No matter how they obtain a meal, all raptors share one important advantage over land animals: they can fly long distances to find food. In tropical and subtropical regions, where food is always available, many raptors patrol large territories all year round. In northern areas, however, raptors often migrate long distances.

One of the world's largest raptor migrations leaves Africa for Europe and western Asia each year. In 1994, in Eilat, Israel, volunteers counted 1,031,387 raptors migrating north— more than 11,000 per day. Just how raptors find their way from one place to another and back again is one of nature's great mysteries. The fact that many raptors follow mountain ranges is a clue that they can read Earth's physical features like a map. But some raptors cross large bodies of water, so they probably also guide themselves by the sun or in other ways that we don't yet understand.

Every year at Hawk Mountain, Pennsylvania, bird-watchers gather to observe about 20,000 raptors flying south for the winter. At least sixteen species take part in these migrations including northern harriers, sharp-shinned hawks, golden eagles, red-tailed hawks, ospreys, and falcons. Some of these birds head for Florida. Others fly to Central and South America, where food is more plentiful during the winter. Several months later, the raptors return north to breed and take advantage of the springtime explosion of insects, rodents, and other prey.

We can learn more about birds of prey by taking a look at the different raptor groups, one by one.

Eilat, Israel is on the route of one of the world's largest raptor migrations. Observers, such as the one shown here, have counted more than 1 million raptors passing by in a year.

The bateleur is one kind of eagle found in Africa.

Chapter Three

Eagles and Ospreys

The name "eagle" has been given to many large raptors, with little regard to their actual relationships to one another. Although ornithologists place all eagles in the same family of raptors, eagles come in many different sizes and behave in many different ways.

About sixty kinds of eagles live on Earth. Both Africa and Asia have a rich variety of eagles. Southern Africa alone

The harpy eagle

has seventeen different eagle species. These include three species of "hawk eagles," four kinds of "snake eagles," five species of "true eagles," and a number of other eagles with names such as "longcrested," "martial," "crowned," and "fish" eagles.

Eagles catch their prey in many ways. The world's most powerful bird of prey is the harpy eagle. This bird nests in the tallest rain forest trees of Mexico, Central America, and South America. With its large size and terrifying talons, the harpy snatches monkeys, sloths, and other animals from the roof of the rain forest.

Other eagles hunt snakes, fish, mammals, and almost any other animal you can think of. Most also eat carrion. The main thing eagles have in common is their large size, but even in that respect, they differ greatly. The harpy eagle, for instance, weighs up to 18 pounds (8 kg), while Africa's booted eagle weighs in at just over 1.5 pounds (0.5 kg). Regardless of size, all eagles are impressive, including the two species living in the United States and Canada.

The Golden Eagle

The golden eagle is one of nine species of large eagles called "true eagles," perhaps because of their enormous sizes and hunting abilities. The golden eagle can be found throughout the Northern Hemisphere and ranks as one of North America's most formidable predators.

With a wingspan of about 7 feet (2.1 m) and a weight of about 10 pounds (4.5 kg), the golden eagle has a large menu of prey to choose from. It prefers open mountainous or hilly country and often hunts rabbits, squirrels, and other small mammals. Golden eagles do sometimes kill larger prey, however.

In Wyoming, biologists often observe golden eagles attacking adult pronghorn antelope several times their size. Usually, an eagle circles about 200 feet (60 m) above a group of pronghorns and then flies away. Moments later the eagle reappears, flying fast and low to the ground. After picking out an antelope, the eagle plunges its talons into its victim's flesh. Sometimes, the antelope falls immediately. Other times, the eagle rides its prey for up to 20 seconds as the antelope tries to run. If the eagle isn't successful on its first try, it continues attacking the antelope until the animal dies.

The golden eagle is a powerful flier and has been known to lift prey as heavy as itself.

Eagles Galore

One of the highest population densities of golden eagles in the United States can be found in the Diablo Range—less than 30 miles (48 km) from the San Francisco Bay Area in California. Here, a large supply of ground squirrels and rabbits allows the eagles to live in unusually small territories.

Public Enemy?

Throughout history, stories of golden eagles snatching babies and killing livestock have made the bird a target of human hatred. Hunters have often shot at eagles for "fun" while ranchers and farmers have trapped them and poisoned them, and even gunned them down from airplanes. At one time, states such as Pennsylvania and Alaska offered bounties for dead eagles, encouraging people to kill hundreds of these magnificent birds.

Today, we know that this slaughter is unjustified. There has rarely, if ever, been a documented case of a golden eagle killing a person. At the same time, golden eagles provide many benefits to people—including ranchers and farmers—by eating rodents and other pests. In some areas such as southwestern Montana, golden eagles do kill lambs, but this is unusual. In such cases, ranchers and game managers have been able to work together to reduce such losses.

Bald Eagles

It's not hard to figure out why the founding fathers of the United States chose the bald eagle to symbolize our nation. With its white head and tail feathers, the bird presents a noble image that reflects our ideals and beliefs. The bird's strength and hunting ability tell other nations that we are ready to defend ourselves. The eagle's soaring grace encourages us to pursue our goals and appreciate the finer things in life.

The national emblem of the United States, the bald eagle, is one of the most well-recognized raptors.

**Sea Eagles:
A Closer Look**

Ten species of sea-eagles live on our planet. Four of them are endangered: the Pallas' fish-eagle and the Solomon, Madagascar, and Stellar's sea-eagles.

Bald eagles or "baldies" belong to a group of eagles known as "sea-eagles." They are more closely related to kites than to the golden eagle. The bald eagle's feet are perfectly adapted for catching fish. Its powerful 2-inch (5-cm) talons are used for stabbing prey. The bottoms of its feet are very rough, and its toes are equipped with sharp **spicules** that help the eagle hang onto its slippery meals.

Bald eagles living in different places hunt different kinds of fish, but all the fish have one thing in common. They live close to the water's surface, where eagles can easily catch them. When necessary, baldies can switch to eating rabbits, rodents, and even other birds. Bald eagles are especially known for **scavenging**. Each year, when salmon spawn in Alaskan rivers, hundreds of baldies show up to feast on the helpless, dying fish. They will also eat a variety of dead animals and even feed in garbage dumps.

DDT Disaster

When Europeans first arrived in North America, the continent was home to between 250,000 and 500,000 bald eagles. Soon, settlers waged war on the birds and shot large numbers of them. People also cut down the trees that the birds nested in and caught large numbers of the fish the eagles needed to survive. Then, in the 1940s, the bald eagle was faced with a new deadly threat—**DDT**.

DDT is an **insecticide**—a poison used to kill insects that people don't like. Beginning in the 1940s, people sprayed DDT and other insecticides all over North America, mostly to kill insects that damaged crops or bit people. These poisons, however, moved through entire **food webs**. Poisons sprayed on insects collected in the bodies of the small birds and fish that ate the insects. It also appeared in the bodies of the small birds and fish that ate the insects. When eagles and other raptors ate the small birds and fish, large amounts of the insecticides became concentrated in the raptors' bodies. The chemicals didn't often kill adult raptors, but they caused the birds to lay eggs with very thin shells. These eggs often broke or failed to hatch. As fewer eggs hatched, the population of bald eagles and many other raptors became alarmingly small.

Fortunately, the United States banned the use of DDT in 1972. Since then, eagle populations have been increasing and, in fact, represent one of the United States' most successful conservation efforts.

The bald eagles in this photograph are hunting for fish along the Platte River in Nebraska. Unfortunately, eating fish has made eagles and other raptors vulnerable to insecticide poisoning.

Today, eagles are seen from southern California to Illinois and Connecticut, often in places where they haven't been seen for decades.

Ospreys

After golden and bald eagles, ospreys are the United States' largest daytime raptors. Ospreys hunt fish and are even better adapted for this way of life than bald eagles. Osprey talons are curved like fish hooks, and the birds are able to bend their outer toes around to the back. With two talons in front and two in back, ospreys can get a better grip on their prey than other daytime raptors.

Ospreys fly above shallow marshes, lakes, or streams looking for fish. When they spot one, the birds dive steeply, sometimes plunging their talons 3 feet (1 m) beneath the water's surface to hook their prey.

Like many other raptor populations, osprey numbers crashed when people began using DDT. In one area of New England, the number of nesting pairs dropped from 150 in 1954 to just 9 in the 1970s. Since the ban on DDT, however,

osprey numbers have quickly increased. People have played a significant role in this recovery, building nesting platforms in many wetland areas. In some places, there are more ospreys today than there were before the DDT years.

Since 1972, when DDT was banned in the United States, the osprey population has made a remarkable comeback.

Red-tailed hawks often build their nests in the crooks of trees. These birds are named after their most noticable feature—their brilliant tail feathers.

Chapter Four

Hawks Harriers, and More

Eagles and ospreys are in the same raptor family as about 140 other daytime birds of prey. These other family members have many different names, such as hawks, goshawks, harriers, buzzards, kites, and Old World vultures.

Buteo Hawks

Many of the raptors that people first encounter are buteo hawks. One of

What Is a Buzzard?

In Europe and Africa, buteos are known as "buzzards," a word people in North America often use incorrectly to describe vultures.

North America's most common buteos is the red-tailed hawk. Its loud "keeee-aaaaaah" pierces the sky in many parts of our continent. Like many other buteos, the red-tail is a large, thick-bodied bird. It has a wingspan of up to 4 feet (1.2 m). Its color varies widely, depending on where it lives, but if you see a soaring raptor with reddish tail feathers, you're probably looking at a red-tail.

Red-tails live throughout North and Central America, a tribute to their adaptability. Where I grew up in southern California, the birds fed mostly on mice and other small mammals. Red-tails in Puerto Rico, however, hunt parrots, lizards, frogs, and other rain forest animals.

Common buteos living in North America include broad-winged, red-shouldered, bay-winged, Swainson's, rough-legged, and ferruginous hawks. Like eagles, buteos usually build large nests high in the treetops. Buteos may be seen almost anywhere, either soaring high above the ground or perched on tall trees and telephone poles. Many migrate long distances every year. Because their wings are built for soaring instead of flapping, they tend to travel along land routes where thermal updrafts of air help carry them from place to place.

Accipiter Hawks

Unlike buteos, the accipiters or "true hawks" have bodies designed for high-speed pursuit. With its short, rounded wings, the accipiter is able to chase its prey through dense woodlands, using its long tail to twist and change directions at

Accipiters, such as the Cooper's hawk, are skillful fliers. They often hunt song birds and other small animals.

high speed. A typical North American accipiter, such as the Cooper's or sharp-shinned hawk, will perch quietly on the branch of a tree until a likely bird victim flies by. Then the accipiter takes off after its target.

Like buteos, accipiters usually build nests in trees. Many also migrate. In 1997, bird-watchers at Hawk Mountain counted 4,218 sharp-shinned hawks migrating south. They also spotted 724 Cooper's hawks and 93 northern goshawks.

Harriers

Harriers or "marsh hawks" are among the most unusual birds of prey. They usually patrol open fields and wetlands. As harriers fly slow and low to the ground, their large wings tilt up in a distinctive V shape. This allows them to glide along on the tiniest breezes and thermals.

Harriers find their prey by sound, as well as by sight. Like owls, their ears are angled forward to collect sound waves. When they detect a small bird or mammal below them, harriers quickly pounce on their victim.

Unlike many other raptors, harriers nest on the ground, usually in marshes or other places where predators aren't likely to reach them. About nine species of harriers live on Earth, but North America has only one—the northern harrier. It is the most **cosmopolitan** of the harriers and can be found on every continent except Australia and Antarctica.

Harriers can be distinguished from other raptors by their owl-like, forward-facing eyes.

Kites

Kites are an especially diverse group of raptors. Five different kinds of kites live in North America: the swallowtailed, Mississippi, black-shouldered, snail, and hook-billed kite. Like harriers, kites fly fairly slowly. Some, such as the black-shouldered kite, are easily recognized by the way they hover

A Rare Raptor

The snail kite is North America's rarest kite. Only about 1,000 live in the United States, all of them in Florida.

above the ground, tirelessly waiting for a mouse or other small mammal to appear below. Others, such as the swallowtailed kite, have a split tail that is clearly visible as they search treetops for food.

Most kites feed on slow-moving prey or carrion. The snail kite of south Florida eats only apple snails. Other kites feed on snakes, rodents, insects, and nestling birds.

Old World Vultures

A group of raptors we don't often hear about in North America is the Old World vultures. Fourteen species of Old World vultures live in Africa, Europe, and Asia. As you might guess, these birds are carrion-feeders. They eat animals that are already dead.

Old World vultures include some of the world's largest flying birds, with wingspans of almost 10 feet (3 m). They sometimes gather by the hundreds to feed on dead zebras, antelope, and other large grazing mammals. Most Old World vultures have unfeathered heads—an advantage for birds that stick their heads into messy carcasses.

Some Old World vultures look like the New World vultures found in North America, but ornithologists place the birds in different scientific groups. Old World vultures are true daytime raptors, related to eagles, hawks, and the other birds in this book. New World vultures such as the turkey vulture, black vulture, and California condor are thought to be more closely related to storks.

Kites build sloppy-looking twig nests. Some lay their eggs on rocky ledges or other natural features while others, such as the swallowtail, nest in the tops of tall trees. In the United States, kites live primarily in the southern, warmer parts of the country and most spend winters in Central or South America. The black-shouldered kite was extremely rare in the early 1900s, but it has adapted well to human development and agriculture. It now lives as far north as Washington state and can be seen fluttering over farms, pastures, and highway median strips in many Sun Belt states.

Even though this caracara looks very different from a falcon, both birds belong to the same family of raptors.

Chapter Five

Caracaras and Falcons

Falcons and their relatives, the caracaras, belong to a different raptor family than the eagles, hawks, and other raptors discussed in Chapters 3 and 4. The falcon family includes about sixty species of raptors—nine caracaras and approximately fifty kinds of falcons.

Caracaras

Caracaras live in the warm regions of North, Central, and South America. They are mostly carrion-feeders, though they usually hunt as well. These large, handsome birds are strong fliers. Eagles, vultures, and other large carrion-feeders often have to wait for warm thermals to develop before they can fly, but caracaras begin searching for food at first light. This early start gives them first pick of animals that have died during the night.

In the United States, crested caracaras are often seen perching on telephone poles along the highways of southern Texas. A smaller population of caracaras lives near Lake Okeechobee in Florida. Here, they find abundant supplies of road-killed opossums, armadillos, and rabbits. In Florida, one naturalist found dozens of turtle shells beneath a caracara nest—proof that caracaras eat a variety of foods.

Falcons

Although caracaras are relatively strong fliers, they look "poky" compared to the other members of their bird family, the falcons. People have admired the falcon's speed and hunting skills for thousands of years. **Falconry**—the practice of using trained falcons or hawks to hunt—began at least 2,750 years ago in the Middle East. Today, as many as 20,000 people worldwide own and train raptors. Many of these trained birds are falcons.

At first, it may seem difficult to tell falcons from eagles, hawks, and other raptors. Falcons have the same curved beaks, the same talons, and many of the same behaviors as other daytime birds of prey. Still, falcons have a look that is all their own. They are generally smaller than most other rap-

Biologist Kate Davis rehabilitates injured and sick raptors. In her free time, she trains raptors for falconry.

Peregrine falcons are skilled hunters. This falcon has just caught a duck.

tors—usually just a bit larger than pigeons. Their short necks and long, swept-back wings help give them that graceful "falcon look," especially when they are flying.

Falcon Feeding

Falcons are especially designed to pursue fast prey. They often catch dragonflies, grasshoppers, and other insects, but they are most impressive when they hunt other birds.

The peregrine falcon has earned a reputation as the world's top bird hunter. Peregrines have many hunting methods, but the most dramatic is the **stoop**. In a stoop attack, the peregrine flies above its victim and then folds its wings and drops like a rocket. Stooping peregrines have been timed at the fastest speeds ever recorded for a bird—more than 200 miles (322 km) per hour.

When it intercepts prey, a falcon slams into its victim with open feet. Sometimes, that first blow is enough to kill the other bird. Unlike eagles and hawks, however, falcons do not often kill their victims by stabbing them with their talons. Instead, falcons use their powerful beaks to quickly cut the victim's spinal cord. A falcon's beak has toothlike **tomial notches** that help this bird deliver fatal "bites" to its prey.

Smart Birds

One thing that impresses people about raptors is how their hunting methods vary according to where they live. Falcons are experts at this. In 1984, an ornithologist watched a newly

Kestrel Confusion

North America's most common falcon, the kestrel, used to be called the sparrow hawk, even though it is not a hawk. Kestrels are found throughout the United States, but often go unnoticed as they sit quietly on telephone lines.

arrived male peregrine pair up with a female in the Yosemite Valley. Although the male had never hunted in Yosemite, within days it had developed a new technique for catching white-throated swifts.

The male would fly along the massive rock face of El Capitan until he spotted a group of swifts. Then he would zip around the corner of the rock face and climb several hundred feet higher into the air. Hidden from the swifts, the falcon then dropped in a 45-degree stoop. Accelerating to speeds of 200 miles (322 km) per hour, he shot back around El Capitan's corner straight into the flock of swifts. In this way, he successfully captured a meal about 80 percent of the time.

Sometimes falcons hunt in groups. Aplomado falcons live in open country with scattered trees. The male does most of the hunting, chasing small birds that it spots from its perch. If one of these birds flees into a bush, however, the male aplomado calls the female. The female then flies or walks into the bush to flush out the victim. As soon as the smaller bird tries to escape, the male aplomado nabs it.

Falcon Reproduction

Unlike most other raptors, falcons do not build nests. Some, such as the aplomado falcon, raise their young in the abandoned nests of other birds. Our most common falcon, the American kestrel, nests in tree holes. Peregrine and prairie falcons prefer to lay their eggs high on rocky ledges, where they are safe from ground predators. Peregrine falcons, in

A female peregrine falcon with her young

fact, are famous for nesting on the skyscrapers and bridges of large cities.

Like other raptors, female falcons are larger than males. After mating, the female tends the eggs and young while the male catches food and helps chase away predators. The young hatch after about 30 days and take flight 30 to 50 days after hatching—a process known as **fledging**.

After fledging, young falcons may stay around the nest site for several weeks or months, improving their hunting and flying skills. Non-migrating falcons may then **disperse**, or spread out, to find their own territories while migrating falcons join adults in their long journeys to winter feeding grounds. The name "peregrine" means "wanderer" or "migrator," and some populations of peregrine falcons undertake incredibly long migrations. Peregrines nesting in northern Greenland fly all the way to the tip of South America and back each year, a round-trip journey of more than 18,000 miles (28,900 km)!

Guarding the Nest

Falcons are known for fiercely defending their nests and their young against much larger birds. In Utah's Zion National Park, a pair of peregrine falcons was seen killing an adult golden eagle that flew too close to their nest!

People Problems

Like other birds of prey, falcons have had their problems with people. In the late 1800s and early 1900s, they were considered a pest by American ranchers, farmers, and gamekeepers.

Many falcons were shot or trapped. Egg collectors also hurt falcon populations by taking the birds' eggs. However, DDT harmed the birds most, especially peregrines and other falcons that specialize in eating birds.

Before World War II, populations of peregrine falcons in the Northern Hemisphere were fairly safe. However, after the use of DDT began, their numbers crashed. By 1964, not a single peregrine falcon nested in the United States east of the Mississippi River. Half of the peregrines in Great Britain and France also disappeared, with even greater losses in other European and Asian countries. Peregrine populations in Africa, Australia, and South America, where DDT was not used so heavily, remained relatively stable.

Populations of peregrine falcons dropped dramatically due to use of DDT.

The Santa Cruz Predatory Bird Research Group has reintroduced peregrine falcons throughout much of the west by releasing young peregrines at "hack sites" such as this one in Point Reyes, California.

Bounce Back

Evidence that DDT led to nesting failure in peregrines was one of the main reasons this insecticide was banned in the United States and Canada. Even before the ban took effect, however, people around the world began working to restore peregrine populations. In 1970, scientists at Cornell University began an active program to breed raptors in captivity and place young birds back into the wild. They created a nonprofit organization called The Peregrine Fund and, by 1995, had succeeded in establishing more than 170 peregrine breeding pairs east of the Mississippi.

In the West, the Santa Cruz Predatory Bird Research Group conducted similar programs. The group has reintroduced the peregrine to many parts of California, Nevada, Arizona, and Oregon. More than 800 pairs of peregrines now breed throughout the West, up from just 19 pairs in the mid-1970s. Programs are also underway to breed and reintroduce other endangered raptors such as the aplomado falcon, Philippine eagle, and harpy eagle.

As tropical forests are cut to make way for farming, raptors and many other birds lose their homes.

Chapter Six

Wings of the Future

Human efforts to restore raptor populations reflect our admiration for these fascinating birds. They also reflect our growing understanding of our environment and the roles different species—including ourselves—play in it.

Unfortunately, raptors are not yet safe. While countries in Europe and North America have banned DDT and other insecticides, many other countries still use these deadly chemicals. In the United States, a whole new crop of chemical poisons now kill millions of birds each year, including eagles and other raptors.

An even greater threat to many raptor species is the destruction of their homes. This is especially true of raptors such as the harpy eagle and Philippine eagle, which live in tropical forests. Both species have disappeared from many places where they once lived, and their numbers continue to decline as tropical forests are logged, burned, and cut down for agriculture.

Dealing with these threats will require a new determination on our behalf and greater research into raptor biology. The success stories of the bald eagle, the peregrine falcon, and the osprey, however, give us reasons to be hopeful that our most spectacular bird hunters will find clear skies far into the future.

Injured, Dead, and Tagged Raptors

Most people will come across an injured or dead raptor sometime in their lives. Sadly, thousands of raptors are injured or killed by colliding with cars, buildings, and telephone wires. Many others are illegally shot or poisoned.

If you find a dead raptor, check to see if it has a band on one of its legs. If it does, carefully write down the number and other information on the band.

Then send this information, along with a precise description of where, when, and how you found the dead bird to:

Department of the Interior
U.S. Fish and Wildlife Service
Bird Banding Laboratory
Laurel, MD 20811

Be sure to include your thoughts on how the raptor may have died and describe any other markings on the bird, such as colored plastic tags. Scientists will use that information to learn more about raptor behavior and protecting raptors.

If you find a sick or injured raptor, call your state fish and game agency or a local animal shelter. They should be able to direct you to a person who knows how to treat and rehabilitate injured birds. If no shelter or raptor specialist is available, try to get the help of an adult, such as a biology teacher or veterinarian, who has experience handling animals. ***Never try to approach the raptor yourself, and keep other people and animals away from the bird until a knowledgeable person arrives.***

Glossary

band—(verb) to place a tag on the leg or other body part of an animal so that it can be identified and tracked.

bird of prey—a raptor; a group of birds that includes owls, eagles, hawks, and falcons. These meat-eating birds hunt other animals for food. The word "prey" is used to describe any animal that is eaten by another animal.

camouflage—any form of disguise that helps an animal blend with its surroundings.

carrion—the flesh of a dead animal.

cosmopolitan—a species or object that can be found in many parts of the world.

DDT—an insecticide that caused dramatic declines of many bird populations, including raptors. Adult birds that ate animals with DDT in their bodies produced thinner shelled eggs. These egg shells broke or hatched too early, killing the developing chicks inside.

disperse—to leave the place an animal is born in order to find and establish its own territory.

falconry—the practice of using trained raptors to hunt game birds and mammals.

fledging—the process of attaining the adult feathers necessary to fly.

food web—the food relationships between communities of plants and animals. Raptors are usually at the top of a food web along with other large predators.

insecticide—a chemical substance used to kill insects. Pesticides are chemical substances used to kill a variety of animal pests, such as insects, mice, and rats.

migrate—to travel from one place to another, usually along a well-defined course and at a specific season or time of year.

offspring—the young produced by a plant or animal.

ornithologist—a biologist who studies birds.

raptor—a bird of prey. Scientists divide raptors into two groups, the owls or "nighttime" birds of prey and the "daytime" birds of prey. The latter group includes such birds as eagles, hawks, and falcons.

scavenging—eating dead animals that were captured and killed by other animals.

specics—a group of organisms that have common characteristics. Members of a species can mate with each other and produce healthy young.

spicule—a hard, tiny barb on the feet of some raptors. Spicules help the birds grasp slippery prey, such as fish.

sternum—an animal's breastbone. It is the attachment point for a bird's flight muscles.

stoop—the steep, fast dive of a falcon or other raptor, often used to capture prey.

talon—one of the nails or claws on the toes of a bird of prey.

thermal—a column of warm air that rises into the sky. A thermal is usually formed when the sun heats up the ground which, in turn, warms the air above it.

tomial notch—a toothlike projection on the beaks of falcons, which helps distinguish them from other birds of prey

To Find Out More

Books

For general information about raptors, try:

Arnold, Caroline. *Hawk Highway in the Sky: Watching Raptor Migration*. San Diego: Gulliver Books, 1997.

Arnold, Caroline. *Saving the Peregrine Falcon*. Minneapolis: Lerner Publications, 1990.

Fourie, Denise K. *Hawks, Owls, and Other Birds of Prey*. Parsippany, New Jersey: Silver Burdett Press, 1995.

Hendrickson, John. *Raptors: Birds of Prey*. San Francisco: Chronicle Books, 1992.

Lang, Aubrey. *Sierra Club Wildlife Library: Eagles*. San Francisco: Sierra Club Books, 1990.

Parry-Jones, Jemima. *Eagle: And Other Birds of Prey*. New York: Alfred A. Knopf, 1997.

Patent, Dorothy Hinshaw. *Eagles of America*. New York: Holiday House, 1995.

To identify raptors, try:
Sutton, Clay and Patricia Taylor Sutton. *How to Spot Hawks and Eagles*. Shelburne, Vermont: Chapters Publishing Ltd., 1996.

Wheeler, Brian K. and William S. Clark. *A Photographic Guide to North American Raptors*. San Diego: Academic Press, 1995.

Organizations and Online Sites

http://www.envirolink.org
This is a useful search engine for anyone trying to obtain information on conservation issues. A search for "raptors" will list a number of other sites that may be helpful.

http://www.peregrinefund.org/PFHome.html
This site discusses the Peregrine Fund's latest conservation projects and priorities, describes the Fund's World Center for Birds of Prey, and provides links to other raptor-related sites.

http://www.info-xpress.com/hawkwatch

Try this site to find out about Hawkwatch, an organization dedicated to monitoring raptor populations in the West and promoting raptor awareness, conservation, and research.

http://www.audubon.org

This site provides general information about bird-watching and bird conservation, including raptors, and provides links to other sites.

http://www.hawkmountain.org

Want to find out how many raptors have migrated past Hawk Mountain this year? Check out this website for the latest numbers and other useful information about North American raptors.

A Note on Sources

Like most authors, I have developed my own routine for researching a book such as this one. The first thing I always do is go to a library. For this book, I headed to the university and public libraries in my hometown of Missoula, Montana, and checked out general books on the topic. These included *Birds of Prey* edited by Ian Newton, *Raptors: The Birds of Prey* by Scott Weidensaul, *African Birds of Prey* by Warwick Tarboton, and *Eric Hosking's Birds of Prey of the World* by Eric and David Hosking. Next, I look at CD-ROM and other electronic databases to find useful articles from scientific journals and popular magazines.

My favorite stage of research comes after reading published books and articles. This is when I speak directly to experts in the field. For this book, I was able to rely on my longtime friend and raptor biologist, Craig Himmelwright, as well as my "newtime" friend, biologist Kate Davis. Both of these people tirelessly answered my questions about raptors and shared their fascinating personal experiences with these remarkable birds. Kate also introduced me to raptors first-hand by allowing me to photograph injured birds of prey that she is rehabilitating.

One final important source for this book was the Peregrine Fund, whose staff answered a number of my questions and provided information for this book. I urge readers to check out this group's website at *http://www.peregrine fund.org/WSites.html.*

Index

Numbers in *italics* indicate illustrations.

About the Author

Raptor Fan **Sneed B. Collard III** is the author of twenty award-winning science and nature books for young people. *Booklist* awarded a starred review to Mr. Collard's recent Franklin Watts book, *Monteverde: Science and Scientists in a Costa Rican Cloud Forest*, describing it as "intoxicating reading." His other titles include *Animal Dads*, *Sea Snakes*, *Animal Dazzlers*, *Creepy Creatures*, and *Alien Invaders: the Continuing Threat of Exotic Species*.

Each year, Mr. Collard travels widely, speaking to thousands of students and teachers throughout the United States. In his free time, he often watches ospreys and eagles near his home in Missoula, Montana. You may contact Mr. Collard by writing to him c/o Franklin Watts, 90 Sherman Turnpike, Danbury, CT, 06816.